THIS WAS AMERICA

Little, Brown & Company   Boston / Toronto

THIS WAS

AMERICA

Martin W. Sandler

BOOKS BY MARTIN W. SANDLER

FOR CHILDREN

The Story of American Photography: An
Illustrated History for Young People

The Way We Lived: A Photographic Record of
Work in a Vanished America

FOR ADULTS

This Was Connecticut: Images of a Vanished
World

This Was New England: Images of a Vanished
Past

TEXTBOOKS

The People Make a Nation

The Restless Americans (with Edwin C.
Rozwenc and Edward C. Martin)

In Search of America

First Edition

Library of Congress Cataloging in Publication Data

Sandler, Martin W
    This was America.

    Based on the television series This was America.
    Includes bibliographical references.
    1. United States—Description and travel—
Views. 2. United States—Social life and
customs—1865-1918—Pictorial works.
I. This was America (Television program)
II. Title.
E168.S22   973.8   80-36853
ISBN 0-316-77022-1

Designed by David Ford

MU
Published simultaneously in Canada
by Little, Brown & Company (Canada) Limited

Printed in the United States of America

FOR CAROL

ACKNOWLEDGMENTS

There are many people at WCVB-TV in Boston who are responsible for the success of the *This Was America* television series. They include president Robert M. Bennett, vice-president Bruce Marson, producer Claude Pelanne, researcher Sherry Reisner, and editor Dave Teixeira. I am particularly indebted to Steve Schlow. As producer and co-writer of the initial programs and as executive producer of the entire series, he has brought his own combination of poetry and genius to the project, and for this I am eternally grateful.

I would like to thank three close friends, Llewellyn Howland III, John Wilmerding, and Dan Jones, for the help and encouragement they have given me in preparing this book.

Space does not allow a listing of the literally hundreds of people connected with museums, libraries, universities, galleries, historical societies, and private collections who helped me in my search for photographs, quotations, anecdotes, and historical information. I would be remiss, however, in not specifically thanking Ellie Reichlin, Shirley Green, Jerry Kearns, Leroy Bellamy, George Hobart, John Kelly, Edith LaFrancis, Cherie Tripp, Tony Decaneas, and Lucinda Burkepile.

I am most grateful to Mary Louise Heinemann for all the work she has done in connection with this book. I would also like to express my appreciation to Susannah Laskaris, Laura Evans, Rosemary Mackenzie, and my friend and conscience, Melissa Clemence.

Finally, there are two very special people to whom I am deeply indebted. David Ford has designed this book with skill and sensitivity that show through on every page. Bill Phillips has contributed his own special blend of patience, dedication, and insight. I owe him much, as both friend and editor.

INTRODUCTION

I know histhry isn't thrue, . . . because it ain't like what I see ivry day . . . if anywan comes along with a histhry . . . that'll show me the people fightin' . . . makin' love, gettin' married, owin' the groceryman and bein' without hard coal, I'll believe it but not befure.

[History] . . . tells ye what a counthry died iv. But I'd like to know what it lived iv.

Finley Peter Dunne

This book tells the story of what America "lived of" during the most important era in the history of this nation. It is, I hope, a very human book: one much more concerned with the feelings and ways of life of a people than with the politics or specific events of the era. It is an attempt to capture through pictures and words the emotions of those whose experiences built America.

American history, like that of every nation, is filled with its share of myths. Generations of schoolchildren, for ex-ample, have been taught that the people most responsible for making Americans what they are today were those whom the textbooks commonly label "the founding fathers." The truth, however, is that very few of us have anything in common with these people. We are what we are because of much more recent ancestors. Our lives have been shaped most directly, not by "founding fathers," but by forefathers who at the turn of this century lived through a period of extraordinary change. It was during this time that the emergence of modern America took place.

It was a remarkable era, made even more remarkable by the fact that there was a whole new way of recording it. In 1900 the camera was still only sixty-one years old. Yet from coast to coast there were people snapping pictures, unwittingly creating a visual tapestry of life in a critical era of American history.

The story of this period is filled with drama, excitement, and suspense. When I was given the opportunity of telling it in a television series, my prime goal was to make the era come alive. In order to do this, I looked at hundreds of thousands of glass negatives and prints. I pored over countless diaries, journals, speeches, and news stories. Above all, I was determined to show the human side: how people looked, how they earned their living, how they spent their day off, and, most important, how they felt.

This book is an outgrowth of the television production. Its six chapters coincide with the first six programs in the series. The first chapter presents an overview of the period and tells the story of four early photographers who chronicled the era in different ways. The chapters that follow describe the ways Americans moved about, worked, played, lived as a family — and changed. The final chapter returns to the photographers and shows how different cameramen and -women presented their own special visions of turn-of-the-century America.

In a television program, scores of still photographs can be used to illustrate a single point. Hundreds of images pass by, creating almost a kaleidoscopic effect. This, of course, cannot be done in a book. Yet there is an important advantage that the print medium has over television: once the photograph is on the page, it is there to stay. The reader can spend as long as he wants with it, studying details, reflecting on something in the picture that has particular personal attraction or meaning.

In creating this book from the television series I became aware that I was facing a whole new set of challenges — and opportunities. As I picked each picture I asked myself such questions as: Does it best illustrate the point? Does it move the story along? Can it be looked at again and again, perhaps each time revealing something new about the period and the people? Converting the television script into a cohesive text was a whole different kind of challenge. As anyone who has worked in both media will attest, writing for the printed page is much different from writing for the spoken word.

The words and pictures in this book are meant to evoke the themes of the daily lives of Americans at the turn of the century. That the text and photographs reveal modes of life different from our own is obvious. Yet it was less than one hundred years ago! How incredible that the onrush of time can separate us so completely from scenes that were recently commonplace. The words and pictures convey the sense of pride, of confidence, of optimism that was so much a part of the period. Today, at a time when we seem to be assailed from all sides, when our values seem to be constantly under attack, we can look back and find much to be proud of in our heritage and the people who made us what we are.

CONTENTS

THIS WAS AMERICA

1

A PHOTOGRAPHER IS COMING

America at the turn of the century. Less than one hundred years ago.

"We are the light of the world," a statesman will say; "we are doing God's work on earth."

Sea Breeze, Florida, 1904   Detroit Publishing Company

A poet writes of songs he can hear rising from the soul of the nation.

Nebraska, 1903   W. A. Raymond

"There is not a man here," says a senator from New York, "who does not feel four hundred percent bigger in 1900 than he did in 1896, bigger intellectually, bigger hopefully, bigger patriotically."

Madison, Wisconsin, 1894   Photographer unknown

Everything seems new;

everything seems possible.

everything seems good;

It is a remarkable time. More than fifty percent of all American workers still earn their living at farm labor of one kind or another, but this will soon be changed. The industrial revolution is altering the way people work, communicate, and live. A handcraft nation of isolated farms and villages is being transformed into an industrial giant of bustling and booming cities.

Worcester, Massachusetts, c. 1910   E. B. Luce

There are great changes taking place in the way people move about. Trolleys, trains, automobiles are all part of an amazing transportation revolution. At the turn of the century, Americans can get to more places more quickly than ever before.

New words are creeping into the vocabulary, words like *leisure*. From the beginning, Americans have looked upon play with guilt and suspicion. Now new ways of working and living bring about the desire for new ways of play. All across the country the day off — and in some cases, the day and a half off — is being spent at places other than the church or the front porch. In ball fields, on beaches, at amusement parks, in grandstands, from coast to coast Americans are learning something new. They are learning to play.

Detroit, Michigan, 1906   Detroit Publishing Company

In the eyes of most Americans it is all
seen as growth and progress: the very
keynotes of the turn of the century. Not
all observers, however, agree. Says one
journalist, "Progress cannot be reck-
oned in railroads and steamboats, or
counted in money or decided in any
way by the census tables. Are we pro-
ducing better children and better men
and women? This is the question which
decides everything."

Newton, North Carolina, 1908   Lewis Hine

The question falls upon deaf ears, for it is an age of remarkable optimism. The Cocksure Era, it will be called.

A Brooklyn minister proclaims, "Laws are becoming more just, rulers more humane; music is becoming sweeter and books wiser."

A United States senator speaks for colleagues and constituents alike when he states, "God has marked the American people as His chosen nation to finally lead in the regeneration of the world. This is the divine mission of America and it holds for us all the profit, all the glory, all the happiness possible to man."

St. Louis, Missouri, c. 1900   Dick Lemen

Location unknown, 1906   Photographer unknown

It is an age of beginnings, a time of promises; and while ministers preach it and statesmen proclaim it holy, others are capturing it in moments, making the age permanent, freezing time so that it will touch Americans long after the glow has faded, long after the promises have been forgotten.

The camera brings about a new way of
seeing the world.

Milford, Connecticut, 1902   T. S. Bronson.

16

It is able to stop time, to record images
of life before they vanish forever.

The camera bursts upon the scene as the most significant changes in all of American history are taking place. It is a wonderful coincidence, a marriage of a remarkable era and a miraculous new way of recording it.

Americans are fascinated by the camera. Theirs is the first era that has the opportunity for visual immortality, and they are determined to take advantage of it. Whenever a photographer arrives on the scene, they are ready to pose. Sticking heads out of windows, perching atop the most unlikely places — wherever they are, they get into the picture.

It is all captured, the work, the movement, the play. Each change is recorded. Changes are taking place so rapidly that those who are living them will use the pictures to confirm that they are all really happening. An era unique in the history of the world is being made permanent on negatives made of glass.

Massachusetts, c. 1900   Photographer unknown

Overleaf: New York City, c. 1895; Detroit Publishing Company

It is a time when the family is the center of American life, and now there are family albums to pass on from generation to generation. Families pose together; memories are preserved. This is what your grandfather looked like. This was your cousin Sarah just after she died. This is the house in which you were born.

The camera records great changes, but it also brings about great changes itself. It alters the self-awareness of the nation. In a time before movies, radio, and television, Americans have been isolated, unaware of what is happening in other parts of the country. Now Easterners see for themselves what the vast new lands in the West look like. Farmers in the Midwest get their first view of life in the big city. The breadbasket of America is revealed. Pictures of people different from any most Americans have ever seen are studied — in one's own living room. Awareness is raised, horizons are expanded — all through the lens of the camera.

Guthrie, Oklahoma, 1889   A. P. Swearingen

It is a cumbersome business, this picture taking. At the turn of the century photography is only sixty years old. Hand-held cameras are still in their infancy. Most photographs are taken with bulky cameras that have to be set on tripods to hold them steady. Negatives are made of glass coated with chemicals upon which the image is captured. The glass plates are fragile and not easy to handle. In the beginning most photographers have to prepare their own plates, take their pictures, and then develop them themselves. Until late in the nineteenth century most glass plates are of the type that have to be developed within fifteen minutes of their exposure. On expeditions to remote places photographers often carry large boxes draped with a dark cloth into which they can crawl in order to "fix" their pictures in time.

The trouble and the bother do not deter them. These early photographers are a special breed. They haul their bulky equipment and heavy plates everywhere. Legends are born: of the photographer who lugs hundreds of pounds of equipment to the top of a mountain, spends three days capturing spectacular scenes, and then loses them all when the mule carrying the equipment slips on the descent and the glass plates are shattered; of the cameraman who spends months recording life on the prairie, goes off on another journey, and returns home to find that unwitting neighbors have peeled the emulsion off all his plates and have used the glass for greenhouses and cold frames.

Most of the photographers are not famous. The ordinary things of an extraordinary time are being recorded by ordinary people who share a passion for freezing the moment. They are professionals and amateurs, men and women, people from all walks of life, and soon they are everywhere. Every city, every town, every hamlet has its own cameramen and -women. They possess varying degrees of talent, but they are all documenting America.

Yosemite, California, c. 1875   Photographer unknown

Black Canyon, Colorado, 1871   Timothy O'Sullivan

Asbury Park, New Jersey, 1906   T. S. Bronson

"There are two things I want to do," says one early photographer. "I want to show the things that need to be appreciated. I want to show the things that need to be corrected." In turn-of-the- century America there are indeed many things to appreciate, and there are many others in great need of correction. Yet these are not the only reasons for taking pictures.

Location unknown, c. 1880 Photographer unknown

The motives of these cameramen and -women are as varied as their subjects. Some set out to capture a lasting record of their town, their kinfolk, their neighbors. Some see in the camera a way to make social comments. Others are spurred on by the desire to make personal statements, to turn their photography into art. Many are motivated simply by the desire for profit.

Location unknown, c. 1905   Clinedinst

Experience has taught Americans that through hard work anything can be achieved. "Profit is the gift God gives a man for work well done," says a New England minister. And it becomes increasingly clear that the camera itself can produce income as well as images.

In Ashfield, Massachusetts, two brothers, George and Alvah Howes, find through the camera a quick way to earn "God's gift of profit." They are odd-job men, contractors, haulers. But they put all that aside to take a camera up and down the Connecticut Valley selling photographs. Their sales pitch is uniquely American and particularly suited to the times. They send an advance man. "A photographer is coming," he says, "to photograph your house or your business for historical purposes. If you'd like to be in the picture, you can stand out in front when he takes it."

Few can resist having their picture taken, and when the Howes brothers come back two weeks later "just to show the picture," few can resist spending the dollar needed to own it. Their history con game earns the Howes brothers a living, pure and simple. But each of the photographs left behind tells us today of life in a time before ours.

These images show us a different America. Labor and effort, work and will dominate. There are few multinational corporations, no energy shortages, no psychiatry. Credit cards can't even be imagined. An automobile is not a totally uncommon sight, but in all of America there are only one hundred fifty miles of paved roads. Refrigerator? Radio? They are things of the future.

Cummington, Massachusetts, c. 1900   George and Alvah Howes

Overleaf: Western Massachusetts, c. 1900; George and Alvah Howes

Somers, Connecticut, c. 1903   George and Alvah Howes

Western Massachusetts, c. 1900   George and Alvah Howes

Western Massachusetts, c. 1900   George and Alvah Howes

Western Massachusetts, c. 1900   George and Alvah Howes

The Howes brothers have a particular talent for capturing images of workers — people who earn their living by the sweat of their brow. Carpenters, cobblers, lumbermen, farmers, icemen, railroad and trolley workers — they are proud of what they are doing and eager to pose for the camera with the tools of their trade.

These people work ten to twelve hours
a day, six days a week. Pride, challenge, and strength are mirrored in
their faces. There they are. The people
whose courage and faith are building
America.

Holyoke, Massachusetts, 1902 George and Alvah Howes

These two traveling photographers say they are historians. It gets them customers. It makes earning "God's gift of profit" much easier. What they do not know is that they are, in fact, documenting part of an era, recording images of a people and a time that will never come again. How ironic that the pictures they leave behind will make them the very historians they pretend to be.

Western Massachusetts, c. 1900   George and Alvah Howes

To the Howes brothers the camera is a working tool. While they use it to make a living, a woman in Washington, D.C., begins to use her camera in a different way. Her name is Frances Benjamin Johnston and she is destined to become one of America's first photojournalists. She moves between two different worlds. A niece of Mrs. Grover Cleveland, she has direct access to high society and to the circles of official Washington. Yet she will spend much of her life taking pictures of people much less privileged than she. She is a unique woman: unique in her life-style, unique in her goals, unique in the very profession she has chosen.

Early in her career she takes a self-portrait. It is a powerful commentary on her skill as a photographer — and on her personal sense of independence. "The woman who makes photography profitable," she says, "must have good common sense, unlimited patience to carry her through endless failures, equally unlimited tact, good taste, a quick eye, and a talent for detail."

37

A talent for detail. As she hauls her equipment around the country, the pictures she takes reveal this special gift. She composes her photographs in such a way that often details within the photograph itself make their own powerful statement. She is a master at creating pictures within a picture.

Washington, D.C., 1899   Frances Benjamin Johnston

Her primary goal is to use the camera, not for profit, but to reveal. She wants to make the nation aware of people, places, conditions they would not otherwise know. She publishes photographic essays of women factory workers. She gives the nation its first view of life aboard Admiral Dewey's Great White Fleet. She chronicles the Washington schools at a time when the world is anxious to see how America's relatively new public-education system is working.

Washington, D.C., 1899 Frances Benjamin Johnston

Tuskegee, Alabama, 1906 Frances Benjamin Johnston

Her most important work is done in the South. Here she uses her camera to reveal a way of life of which most Americans are totally unaware. She photographs black students at Tuskegee and Hampton institutes. These are young people, "up from slavery," eager to learn a trade, eager to make a better life for themselves and those who will follow them. Her photographs capture the dedication, the determination — and the irony.

Tuskegee, Alabama, 1906   Frances Benjamin Johnston

42

There is a dignity present in the images she provides of the rural black South. Hers is the documentary camera at its best, creating awareness through pictures taken with talent and sensitivity.

She spends the next quarter century traveling across the country, photographing the rich, the poor, the powerful, and the powerless. "I've learned not to depend on the Lord," she says; "I'll make the changes myself." It is a lesson the nation will be learning for years to come.

Washington, D.C., 1902   Frances Benjamin Johnston

For Frances Benjamin Johnston, the camera is a tool with which to make social statements. For the Howes brothers, it is a livelihood. In New Haven, Connecticut, there is a photographer who uses his camera for still another purpose. His name is T. S. Bronson. He is a successful medical doctor. He is also a talented photographer. He takes his pictures with a definite purpose in mind: he wants to celebrate life.

His subjects are primarily members of the newly emerging and confident American middle class. They are what America will hope to become in the decade ahead. They are proud. Pride becomes less of a sin every day as the nation begins to show its industrial muscle. These people know that things can only go forward. A cataclysmic war? Something for Europe, maybe, but not here. This is the Promised Land.

Mt. Carmel, Connecticut, 1909   T. S. Bronson

Orange, Connecticut, 1906   T. S. Bronson

By the age of thirty, T. S. Bronson owns forty cameras. By the age of forty he has taken more than thirty-five thousand photographs. He has become a serious and appreciated photographer. In fact, he spends more time with the camera than he does with the stethoscope. Finally he admits his fate; he gives up medicine to devote his life to photography.

New Haven, Connecticut, 1906   T. S. Bronson

There is an ease about his photographs,
a gentleness. His eye is sensitive to the
meaning beyond the moment. He gives
us images that are personal statements.
He records an era:

its play;

Westbrook, Connecticut, 1908   T. S. Bronson

its work;

Seymour, Connecticut, 1901   T. S. Bronson

its movement.

New Haven, Connecticut, c. 1900   T. S. Bronson

Most important of all, he shows us the
people, caught in a time when they
know they are being recorded for pos-
terity. Bronson captures a feeling of
hope that we cannot imagine. Hope and
promise — the essence of turn-of-the-
century America.

Milford, Connecticut, 1904   T. S. Bronson

2

ON THE MOVE

Promontory, Utah, May 10, 1869. Four years after the Civil War, the dream of westward expansion by rail, begun in 1850, becomes a reality with the driving of the golden spike. East and West have been united. Time has been conquered by steam power. Space has been conquered by the labor and lives of experts and engineers, railmen and sledge swingers, cooks and coolies. The six-month coast-to-coast journey by boat is reduced to seven days by rail. The continent is made smaller by two bands of steel.

It is not surprising that so much effort, so much publicity have gone into the linking of the rails. The railroad is the very symbol of motion, and in America freedom is measured by the ability of an individual to move on, pack up and go, find new horizons. Motion is at the very center of the American character.

Promontory, Utah, 1869   A. J. Russell

It is in the cities that motion is most apparent, and in the beginning most of the
motion is made possible by the horse.
Cities are crowded with horses and the
vehicles they pull. If something must be
transported, it is transported by horse,
and nearly everything is transported,
including people.

The horse is silent witness to the business of the nation. Major cities have horse-drawn trolleys to move office workers and shoppers. Horses pull ambulances. They are an important part of fire-fighting teams.

They are particularly vital in rural areas. Although machinery is steadily changing the whole nature of farming, much of the work is still carried on by horse power. On the prairies of Kansas and Nebraska horses dominate the landscape.

Overleaf: Kansas, c. 1890; photographer unknown

Even relaxation is taken at three miles an hour. Family outings, courtship, and sightseeing take place in coaches and buggies in parks and along tree-lined streets all across America.

Chicago, Illinois, c. 1905   Detroit Publishing Company

But motion is dependent on steady power. Profits can be measured by the time it takes to earn them. The horse works at its own pace, and its pace is soon outstripped by that of the nation.

Science is already providing new and more steady sources of power, and it is in the city that they are first put to use. It is in the city that the horse first becomes obsolete.

Buffalo, New York, c. 1900   Detroit Publishing Company

In Richmond, Virginia, an engineer and former employee of Thomas Edison begins operating the first successful electric transport system in the nation. His name is Frank Sprague. The date is February 2, 1888. Before 1900, every major East Coast city will find itself building and operating an electric surface-transport system.

Dependable power. Speed. Comfort. The trolley moves between cities as well as within them. Soon in every region of the country there is an interconnecting network of tracks that makes it possible to travel great distances by trolley. Cleveland to Akron. Sacramento to Los Angeles. There is even serious talk of building a trolley line from Chicago to New York — a distance of some eight hundred miles. The streetcar, as it is also called, becomes a matter of civic pride. Public transportation symbolizes economic growth, urban security, and citizen comfort.

Hampton Beach, New Hampshire, c. 1905   Photographer unknown

By the turn of the century there are fifteen thousand miles of track and thirty thousand trolley cars. City dwellers travel to areas that are as new and exciting to them as the distant capitals of Europe. At the end of the lines, smart trolley owners build amusement parks and beach areas. Now there are even more compelling reasons to take the trolley, and weekend use nearly equals that of the workweek.

The nation begins its first romance with a machine, and finds a new hero — the motorman. A regular visitor to the neighborhood, known by his first name to both adults and children, the man who runs the trolley finds himself in a position of romance and trust usually reserved for fictional characters. And he knows it. "You see the sunshine and the flowers," the motorman's handbook states. "You are out among the people and have an idea of what the world is doing." If Americans love the machine, they love even more the man who runs it.

Mt. Carmel, Connecticut, 1901   T. S. Bronson

Washington, D.C., c. 1895   Photographer unknown

The trolley brings changes to the landscape along with the tracks, wires, and amusement parks. Real-estate developers are quick to realize that the city can expand outward. Commuting by electric power is convenient and the system is reliable. Not long after the trolley's arrival, cities begin to be surrounded with a new kind of community, one free of industry and crowding, one that suits the need for space: the suburb.

But the trolley is tied to its rails. There are streets it does not travel; lanes it can only pass; vistas it will never see. There is another kind of transportation, one that is personal and controlled, convenient, and unlimited by terrain, power source, or temperament. It is the bicycle, and it suddenly appears in suburb and city after having been little more than a curiosity for almost one hundred years.

Manchester, New Hampshire, 1901   Worthington Cornell

Nearly everyone can learn to ride a bicycle and nearly everyone does. In 1885 there are fifty thousand cyclists peddling around the country. By 1895 there are ten million. Play with the bicyle enthralls the nation. Bicycle clubs, often called Wheelmen's Associations, are formed in practically every city and town. Excursions by bike become commonplace. Bicycle races are soon an important part of the sporting scene. No parade is complete without its contingent of cyclists.

Like the horse before it, the bicycle enters into the world of work as well as play. It is an age in which the telegram is the most rapid and dependable form of long-distance communication, and telegrams are delivered by bicycle. Policemen find in the cycle a new and convenient way to cover their beat. In some places even the mail is delivered by bike.

Washington, D.C., c. 1910   Harris and Ewing

Trolley owners, suddenly threatened, see cycling as a nuisance and perhaps a dangerous pastime. But a noted medical journal does not agree.

"The bicycle," it states, "is a release for tension and a cure for anxiety, headache, neuralgia, and hysteria." A New York journalist sums it up: "The 'bike' fills a moral void in city life," he writes.

Upstate New York, c. 1895   N. L. Stebbins

"With his wheel at hand, there is no hard-driven clerk who may not look forward each day to a comforting flight from the daily grind — through the park, along the Hudson and away to pleasant country places.

"Nothing can compare to the wheel as a leaven for the heavy lump of joylessness in our streets," he concludes. For restless America, ideology and motion meet in the bicycle.

Arlington, Virginia, c. 1895   Detroit Publishing Company

By the turn of the century the bicycle and the trolley are as much a part of America as the horse was before them. They are the means and expression of the nation's pace and restlessness. Yet there is another machine that reflects the country's mobile character. "If God had been a fish," Herman Melville wrote, "he would have been a whale." By the turn of the century it might be said that had the Creator been a machine, he would have been a locomotive.

The railroad becomes such an important means of transportation in America that even time is changed. In 1883, the Department of Transportation establishes fixed time zones across the United States. Clocks can no longer be set at the whim of the individual, at the pleasure of city or town. Trains — and the nation — now run on standard time.

Railroad transportation is so central to the commerce of the nation that it quickly becomes more of a necessity than a novelty. Carrying goods and services across the continent, the train becomes the symbol of progress, as well as of motion.

Nevada, c. 1910   J. W. Walker

The push west is ruthless and demanding: ruthless to the land and demanding
of the men who build and finally oper-
ate the ever-growing network of tracks,
junctions, and terminals. Immigrants
from East and West, cheap labor from
China and Europe, men with dreams
give their lives so that a shipment of
beef cattle from Omaha may arrive in
New York or Boston in six days.

Weber Canyon, Utah, 1868   A. J. Russell

Trains can move people as easily as they can move cattle or steel. With the closing of the frontier made official in 1890, the nation directs its forces inward. The new land is no longer new, but it is still full of promise. The American family begins to gain a continental dimension. Immigrants now settled in Pittsburgh, having left their parents in Serbia, find that they must travel to Dubuque if they are to see their grandchildren.

The train station becomes a temple of greetings and farewells, laughter and tears. The train becomes both a means to the pleasures and an escape from the pains of life. Lovers reunite by train. Jobs lost in one city can be regained in another. Hopes are rekindled at the sound of the whistle. Memories are released at the turn of a curve.

How often are children to wait at depots for favorite aunts, grandmothers, or cousins? How many summers have happy beginnings in smoke and steam? And end in the click of the rails?

Haines Corners, New York, c. 1900 Detroit Publishing Company

For the railroad men in their eastern offices, life is one triumph after another — with a few "minor" disappointments, some of which defy explanation.

But the derailment at Chatsworth, the wreck of the '97, and finally the fatal error of Casey Jones only add to the legend steam is writing across the continent. At the turn of the century the railroads are both the nerves and the muscle of the nation.

Barre, Vermont, c. 1900   Photographer unknown

But as early as 1897 there are rumors.
Stories of yet another way of getting
around. Stories about something some
bicycle makers have been working on.
Something so new that they can't quite
name it.

It is part bicycle —

part carriage —

and part something else.

Internal combustion, they call it. Infernal combustion, it seems: noisy, unpredictable, untrustworthy. It is a toy, something to tinker with on Sunday afternoons. It promises little and in the beginning lives up to this promise. It is hard to imagine how profoundly it will affect the nation.

Chicago, Illinois, c. 1895   Photographer unknown

But it moves under its own power, without rails or something to pull it. In Springfield, Massachusetts, Charlie Duryea names his machine the Phaeton Buggy. Out in Michigan Henry Ford names his the Quadracycle. The newspapers call them "horseless carriages."

St. Johnsbury, Vermont, c. 1901   Photographer unknown

New Haven, Connecticut, 1907   T. S. Bronson

At first they belong to the rich. Hand-crafted, machine by machine, they reflect elegance rarely associated with technology. They carry a price — three to twelve thousand dollars — well beyond the average reach.

At Princeton University the president of that institution, Woodrow Wilson, declares, "Nothing has spread socialistic feeling in this country more than the use of the automobile. To the country men they are a picture of the arrogance of wealth, with all its independence and carelessness."

New London, Connecticut, c. 1910   T. S. Bronson

He speaks for the minority. In 1895 there are four automobiles registered in the state of New York. By 1901, the number has risen to more than fourteen thousand. No single invention — not the electric light, not the phonograph, not even the locomotive — captures the American imagination like the automobile.

On Sundays, boys and men walk the roadways and compete to identify cars by name type: Oldsmobile, Reo, Stanley, Hupmobile, Winton Packard, Pope-Hartford, Haynes Apperson, Locomobile. There are more makes of cars than there are breeds of horses. Every machinist can become a manufacturer; every motorist, a mechanic.

Grand Rapids, Michigan, c. 1905   Photographer unknown

In 1898 the assembly line and the Model T are introduced. Henry Ford calls his Model T the universal car. Built to standardized plans with interchangeable parts, it is as elegant and efficient a form of personal transport as a person could want. Inexpensive — a fender costs only two dollars — easy to maintain, and efficient, it is this car and its imitators that finally free the horse from the burden of its labors. A horse-and-buggy land is about to be transformed into a mobile, modern nation.

As the train did before it, the automobile creates new industries in less than a decade. Those of petroleum, rubber, glass, and steel all thrive on the Sunday trip, the weekend excursion, the daily commute. The car gains full acceptance in music halls and country fairs. "I understand you just bought a Ford," a popular joke starts. "Yes," is the reply; "I saw seven of them chasing one pedestrian the other day, and I decided I was on the wrong end of the sport."

By 1910 the "sport" is to be taken seriously. A novelty only ten years before, automobiles are now a common sight on streets and dirt roads throughout the nation. They will change the face of the land and the way Americans live more profoundly than any other machine in history. Before the new century is a decade old, the automobile, and the trucks, buses, wagons, and sight-seeing vehicles adapted from it, replaces the train as the symbol of progress.

St. Louis, Missouri, c. 1900 Dick Lemen

New York City, 1904 Detroit Publishing Company

For a people so in love with motion, it seems the ultimate has been achieved. In 1902 a journalist proclaims, "Our people can move about more quickly and in more ways than at any time in the history of the world. Let us have the intelligence to realize our fortune and to concentrate our efforts on building lives based on thankfulness and humility." But this is America at the turn of the century, a time of growth and progress, a time of hope and promise.

In motion, as in almost everything else,

Grand Canyon, Arizona, c. 1910   Photographer unknown

there are no ultimates — only horizons.

Galveston, Texas, c. 1910   H. B. Morris

WORK AND THE GOSPEL OF WEALTH

"I am the people," a poet wrote, "the mob, the crowd, the mass. Do you know that all of the great work of the world is done through me?" At the turn of the century work is very much at the heart of the nation's life. Labor and effort have always been the avenues to success in America. There has always been more than enough work for everyone. Now, in an age when progress is the keynote, work becomes more important than ever before.

Mississippi River, 1906   Detroit Publishing Company

Much of the work is still done on the farm. In 1890 more than fifty percent of all American workers are engaged in farm work of one kind or another. In the face of an industrial and technological revolution, the farm remains the backbone of the nation.

Farming allows a family to retain its individualism, its privacy, its quiet, its order. Oneness with the earth, reassurance in nature's cycles — these are qualities that remain important to millions of individuals despite burgeoning cities and the industrial age.

Berkeley County, West Virginia, 1910   Smith Brothers

Yet, the coming years will not treat the farmer well. He will be the victim of prolonged droughts. Factors beyond his control will drive his prices down drastically. The lure of new kinds of jobs in the growing factories and offices and the excitement of life in the new big cities will draw sons and daughters away from the farms by the millions.

Location unknown, c. 1910   H. T. Mitchell

In spite of all this, however, the notion of the yeoman farmer remains much more than a myth. It is the farmer who feeds the world, and the lyrics of a popular song of the day reveal the innermost feelings of those who remain rooted to the soil.

There are too many people
Who from their duty shirk
Who'd rather make a fortune
By some other means than work
The man who plants tobacco
Corn, wheat, or cotton now
Is King among the money'd men
He follows up the plow.

Location unknown, c. 1900   Photographer unknown

Shrewsbury, Massachusetts, c. 1890 Photographer unknown

Not only farmers but American workers in general have always found purpose and pride in their work, work that is still carried on to a large degree by age-old methods. At the turn of the century America is a nation where those who work with their hands still outnumber the rapidly growing ranks of industrial workers.

Three-quarters of a million miners toil miles underground, scooping out the coal that will power industries and heat homes and businesses. Theirs is a terribly dangerous existence. Nearly three thousand miners are killed in accidents every year.

Thousands of lumberjacks are at work, chopping down the forests of America. In an era when most homes and stores are made of wood, trees by the millions are cut down and turned into lumber. They are not replaced. Who can imagine a time when America will run short of trees?

Cascade Mountains, Washington, c. 1905 Darius Kinsey

In 1890, there are more than a quarter of a million blacksmiths in the United States. In towns and cities the "smithy" works at his forge and anvil, shoeing the horses that move people and goods, making by hand countless products such as pots and pans, nails and iron plows.

Norwalk, Connecticut, 1902   George and Alvah Howes

Quarry workers, too, rely on might and
muscle to haul out the stone that will be
used to erect private and public buildings.

Western Massachusetts, c. 1900   George and Alvah Howes

Northampton, Massachusetts, c. 1895   George and Alvah Howes

And despite all the mechanical innovations, it is still a time when teamsters and peddlers dominate the American landscape. In 1890 there are more than fifteen million horses in the United States. Teamsters and their wagons make almost all the short-haul deliveries and carry much of the long-distance freight as well.

Western Massachusetts, c. 1900   George and Alvah Howes

Peddlers and their horse-drawn vehicles are a common sight in every city and town. Meat, vegetables, ice, coal — products of all kinds are sold door-to-door by workers who spend six days a week delivering their goods and the seventh tending to the needs of their horses.

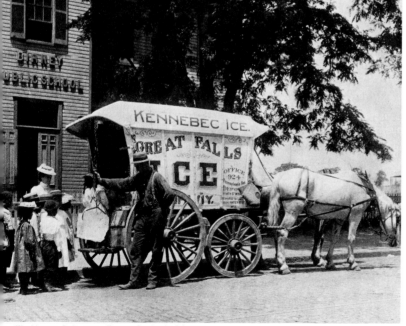

Washington, D.C., 1899   Frances Benjamin Johnston

Boston, Massachusetts, c. 1900   W. K. Watkins

Work in America is not confined to the land. The nation has been built by hard physical labor, and that labor also takes place away from the shore. At a time when there is menace in every change of the wind, peril in each bank of fog, thousands of American fishermen earn their living from the sea. Ports like Gloucester and Boston are jammed with high-masted fishing schooners as fishermen prepare for their journey or unload their catch.

Thousands of other Americans answering the age-old call to the sea earn their living sailing the multimasted commercial vessels that carry coal, lumber, and ice to ports throughout America and as far away as the Caribbean. America's maritime commerce is still dominated by workers who depend upon wind, tide, and canvas.

But it is all changing, for in a land of progress few things remain constant. In a land of ingenuity and innovation nothing changes more dramatically than the world of work.

Portland, Maine, c. 1895   Detroit Publishing Company

By the time the nineteenth century is over, whole new industries have been created; whole new jobs have been born.

Above all else there is the very symbol of the age — the machine. It turns out goods in numbers that stagger the imagination. At the turn of the century the machine increasingly dominates the working habits of the labor force.

Dayton, Ohio, c. 1900   Detroit Publishing Company

Millions of Americans find employment in the factories and mills that house the machines. "I went to work in what is called a factory," says one worker. "I get up at half past five every morning. I get to the factory at six o'clock. The machines go like mad all day. Some- times in my haste I get my finger caught and the needle goes right through it. I bind the finger with a piece of cotton and go on working. We all have accidents like that. I am getting good at the work. By next year I will be making seven dollars a week."

Macon, Georgia, 1909   Lewis Hine

American factories turn out goods at a rate never dreamed of. Dresses, suits, shirts, blouses, coats are mass-produced, and it becomes increasingly difficult to determine people's status in life simply by the clothes they wear. Washing machines, electric stoves, and irons make the life of the American housewife easier. Machines make other machines — harvesters, locomotives, automobiles — that will alter forever the way Americans move and live.

As industries grow, new types of businesses are created that need office and clerical workers to handle the accounts and keep the records, white-collar workers to send out the bills, check the inventories, tally the profits.

Kansas City, Missouri, c. 1910 V. O. Williams

Change in the way a nation works. There are changes that create new jobs, and changes that alter the way old jobs are carried out. It is an age of ingenuity, and now the new industries and businesses spawn new inventions.

Between 1860 and 1890 about one and a half million patents are issued. In every field of endeavor inventions transform old processes. The electric light, the telephone, the telegraph, the mechanical reaper, the sewing machine, the cash register, the fountain pen — each month seems to bring about a new device, a new method that will alter ways of working.

The changes can be seen perhaps most dramatically on the farm. Increasingly machinery replaces hand labor. Between 1880 and 1900 the production of American corn and wheat doubles.

But there are problems. Where will the farmer get the money with which to pay for the new machinery? What will happen to the workers being replaced by the machines?

The changes take place at sea as well. By 1900 steam-powered vessels are replacing those powered by the wind. Sailors need to learn new skills. New ways of work have to be adapted to in an occupation as old as the nation itself.

Boston, Massachusetts, c. 1900   Detroit Publishing Company

As the changes take place, as goods pour out of the factories, as new businesses are created, it becomes obvious that more and more workers are needed. Where will they come from?

"Mother and I came by steerage," says a young Polish immigrant. "We sailed on a steamship in a very dark place that smelled dreadfully. There were hundreds of other people packed in with us: men, women, and children, and almost all of them were sick. But at last the voyage was over and we saw the big woman with the spikes in her head and the lamp that is lighted at night in her hand."

Overleaf: New York City, c. 1900; photographer unknown

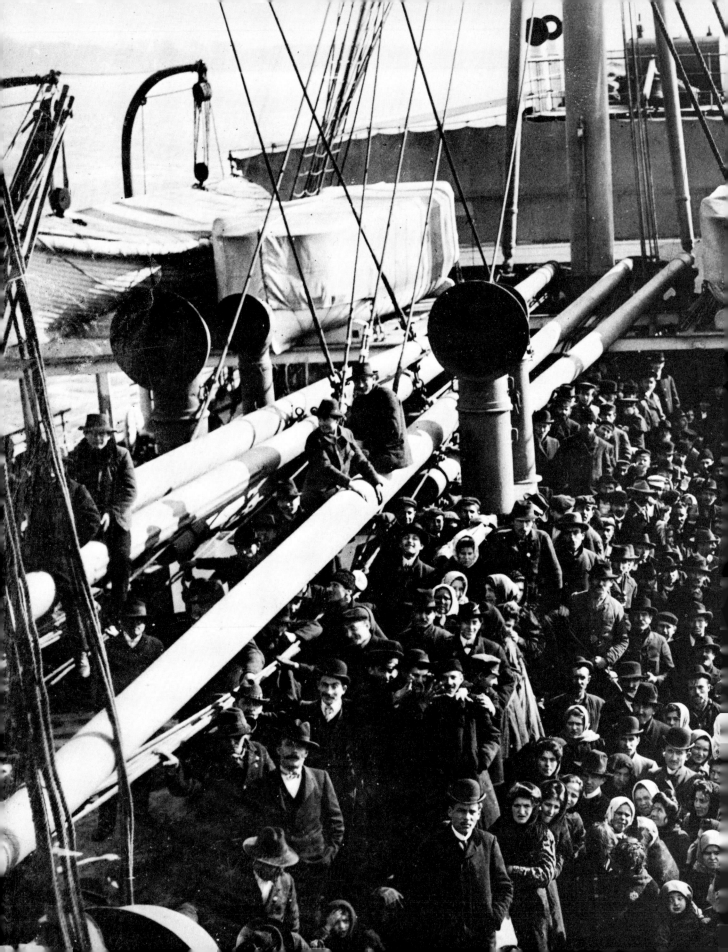

Ellis Island, New York, c. 1910   Joseph Kossuth Dixon

At the turn of the century, the American labor force is unique in the history of the world, for included in the more than thirty-three million workers are some nine million men, women, and children who are new to the nation. Immigrants come in search of a better way of life. They bring their dreams and hopes to a land where opportunities now seem endless, progress limitless, and the ideal attainable.

"I lift my lamp beside the golden door," says the inscription on the Statue of Liberty. To this "golden door" come many so poor that they can hardly scrape together the steerage fare — as low as twelve dollars for the passage from Italy to New York. But come they do, to an America where workers are needed, to an America where they hope that the ideals and the opportunities of democracy will give them a new start in life.

What they find tests their faith — and their courage. Few know the language; few have the occupational skills to qualify them for more than the most menial tasks. "Give me your tired, your poor, your huddled masses yearning to breathe free," says the Statue of Liberty. Others have different points of view. "The immigrants," says Francis A. Walker, president of the Massachusetts Institute of Technology, "are beaten men from beaten races, representing the world's failures in the struggle for existence. They have none of the ideas and aptitudes which belong to those who are descended from the tribes that met under the oak trees of old Germany to make laws and choose leaders."

Barre, Vermont, c. 1895   Photographer unknown

He, and those who think like him, could not be more wrong. The immigrants, arriving at a critical time in the nation's history, will build America. The newcomers work twelve hours a day, six or seven days a week. They work in the factories of New York, in the mills of New Bedford and Fall River, in the coal mines of Pennsylvania, in the slaughterhouses of Kansas City and Chicago, on the farmland of Kansas and Nebraska. They lay tracks for the ever-expanding railroad lines in the West.

Deadwood, North Dakota, 1888   J. S. Grabill

123

St. Louis, Missouri, c. 1900   Dick Lemen

Many find work as domestic servants. It is a time when a family need not be affluent in order to afford a maid or someone to care for the children. It is a time also when the guarantee of three decent meals a day and a clean, comfortable room of one's own is a strong incentive to accept employment in someone else's house, particularly if one is a newcomer to America. By 1900 more than one and a quarter million women work as domestic servants. It is an occupation whose workers are second in number only to those employed in farm labor of one kind or another.

"Genius cannot describe, nor the public mind appreciate what growth has taken place in the United States in the last one hundred years," proclaims the president of the Society of Industrial Mechanics. All across the nation a new phrase, a new philosophy of the time, is articulated, one that will, for many Americans, symbolize the era itself. It is termed the Gospel of Wealth. Says one minister, "It is your Christian Godly duty to attain riches." To most Americans it seems a golden time of profit, progress, unlimited horizons. "In our labor and our victories," says one orator, "we find scope for all our energies, renown enough for all our fame."

Washington, D.C., c. 1895   Photographer unknown

Others see it differently. Says one noted social commentator, "Discovery upon discovery and invention after invention have neither lessened the toil of those who most need respite nor brought plenty to the poor." There is a price for progress, and it is paid particularly by a staggering percentage of the nation's young.

In an age when there are no child-labor laws, children, as young as eight years old, work ten to twelve hours a day, six days a week. There are millions of them. They are one-fifth of the labor force of the nation. They know the sixty-hour week as well as their parents do. They know the loom and the mill, the coal and the cotton. They know the company store and they know the company rules.

They shuck oysters for five cents a pail. In a ten-hour day, a youngster can perhaps fill one and a half pails as the shells slice deep into fingers and cut small hands to ribbons.

Lancaster, South Carolina, 1908   Lewis Hine

Location unknown, c. 1910   Lewis Hine

"The factories need the children," says one tycoon, "and the children need the factories." The child works like the parents: for money, no matter how little. "It is your Christian Godly duty to attain riches," says the "Gospel." So the children work beside their fathers and mothers. Some will die at the machine. Most will not. Few question the world in which they find themselves.

Like their parents, like the office workers, like the men who make the plans and bank the profits, they are too busy. They have no time for questions. There is more coal to sort, another bobbin to fill, another basket of produce to sell. They live life as they find it. They find it hard.

It is all summed up in the lyrics of a song of the day:

The golf links are so near the mill
That almost every day
The laboring children can look out
And see the men at play.

There are others, besides the young, who have paid the price of progress. While many, in the wake of the incredible industrial expansion, have become rich, others are living in situations that can only be described as desperate. Indeed, at no time in the history of the United States is the gap between the rich and the poor as startling as it is at the turn of the century.

New York City, c. 1910   Underwood and Underwood

New York City, 1900   Joseph Byron

Belle Isle, Michigan, c. 1905   Detroit Publishing Company

Most Americans, however, are neither very rich nor very poor. They are part of the rising middle class and for them it *is* a time of unparalleled opportunity. The standard of living in the nation is higher than anywhere else and at any time in the history of the world. There are more goods, more services, more chances for employment than anyone could ever have imagined.

There are more kinds of jobs than were ever thought possible. More than half a million people earn their living in the building trades. As the economy of the nation spirals upward, there is a seemingly insatiable demand for new houses, new offices, new buildings of every kind. City streets are filled with signs advertising the services of carpenters, masons, plumbers, glaziers.

It is an era of progress;   an era of efficiency;

New Orleans, Louisiana, c. 1900   Photographer unknown

above all, an era of unrelenting change.   Some marvel at the changes.

Some never know they are taking place.

Black Hawk Canyon, Colorado, 1898   Keystone Views

Few really understand them.

Belpre, Kansas, c. 1910   W. O. Durstine

And with reason. Look at what has happened. In 1870 there is no such thing as an electric light. By 1900 forty percent of the nation is served by electricity. In 1870 there is no such thing as an electric trolley car. By 1900 there are fifteen thousand miles of trolley tracks in the United States. In 1870 there is no such thing as a telephone. By 1900 there are one and a half million telephones throughout the nation.

Atchison, Kansas, c. 1905 Bendholtz

American workers at the turn of the
century: proud, confident, and perhaps
a bit bewildered. Proud of what has
been accomplished; confident that
things can only go forward; bewildered
by the changes that have taken place.

Washington, D.C., 1879   Photographer unknown

LEARNING TO PLAY

Sunday in turn-of-the-century America — a time for rest, a time for contemplation, a time for glorifying God. After church there is time for the family and friends. It is all time away from the job. On Sunday, like the Lord, you rest, and while you rest you instruct your children to be industrious; to find purpose in their lives; to waste no time; to fight the temptation of idleness.

Americans, schooled in the Puritan ethic, have been taught to believe that work is its own reward. They are uncomfortable with, and often guilty about, the time that machines have freed them to explore. Life can't be lived on the front porch. But is it right to exchange idleness for the pursuit of pleasure? For many the day off and the front porch are practically synonymous.

"We may divide the struggle of the human race into two chapters," President Garfield says. "First there is the fight to get leisure. And the second great fight. What shall we do with our leisure once we have it?"

Location unknown, c. 1895   J. A. Lorenz

143

Palm Beach, Florida, 1904   Detroit Publishing Company

By 1880 many Americans are beginning to realize that the first chapter of humanity's struggle has been completed. A few are well into the second. One learns to enjoy free time when one is rich, and at the turn of the century some Americans are very rich indeed.

They congregate in Newport and Palm Beach, Saratoga and South Hampton. They turn play into an art and make proper amusement a sign of status.

They transform hundreds of acres of beachfront into gardens and call seventy-room mansions "cottages." They make games like golf and tennis their own. They keep stables of horses, dozens of servants, automobiles, and at least one yacht. Says one member of their society, "We keep all we can, except the Ten Commandments."

Newport, Rhode Island, c. 1900   Photographer unknown

They also keep to themselves. "You can do business with anybody," says J. P. Morgan, "but you can only sail a boat with a gentleman." Morgan sticks to his creed. He rarely sails with more than three companions — not counting, of course, his eighty-five-man crew.

Long Island Sound, c. 1895   Charles E. Bolles

Most Americans are not rich, but their life-styles and values are changing nevertheless. Carefully and simply they begin to find joy in the time left over after the six-day workweek.

Gay Head, Massachusetts, c. 1890   Baldwin Coolidge

It is difficult at first. If the rich are at
ease with their time away from work,
those who are not rich are not.

Always there is the sense of duty; the
feeling that pleasure itself has no worth;
the knowledge that time is being
wasted.

Maine, c. 1890   John S. Wright

Voices of warning are heard. "You cannot serve God," preaches a minister,
"and skylark on a bicycle."

But increasingly, free time is filled with
pleasurable activities. And each year
seems to bring more free time.

Actually, there *are* amusements in America that, for over a century, have been acceptable. There have been holidays, for example, since colonial times; holidays and parades. Americans love parades. In the cities, in the towns, in remote rural areas, every excuse possible for staging a parade is seized upon.

At a time when there are few opportunities for relaxation and celebration, Americans find in the parade a chance to dress up, show off, put aside the cares of the job.

Hundreds march or ride; thousands of others watch. The parade is one of the earliest ways in which Americans can get together with their families and friends for pure enjoyment.

Hartford, Connecticut, 1906   T. S. Bronson

Other early forms of recreation are acceptable as well: church socials, religious festivals, and country fairs. Americans love fairs almost as much as they love parades. The exhibits, the food, the chance to see new sights, meet new people — all combine to make the fair, like the parade, a very special occasion.

Special occasions, yes, but there begin to be more and more of them. New in America are the shorter workweek and the shorter workday. By 1900 the workweek has been reduced to five and a half days. For many people the working day has been shortened to nine hours and is heading toward eight. As weekends away from the job become more common and as free time during the week is increased, men, women, and children begin to step out of the routine of their lives. Soon special events begin to attract crowds wherever they are held. Slowly but surely Americans leave the front porch as they reach out for amusement and entertainment.

Concord, New Hampshire, 1894   Photographer unknown

Overleaf: Revere, Massachusetts, 1901; photographer unknown

The Dakotas, c. 1890 H. R. Fair

New Haven, Connecticut, 1908 T. S. Bronson

Wisconsin, 1900 Worthington Cornell

One of the first places they discover is the out-of-doors. The American landscape provides a rich and varied setting for escaping the compression of the factory, the turmoil of the city, the demands of daily life.

Camping, skating, hiking, canoeing — all become increasingly popular. Fishing trips are organized. Hunting clubs are formed.

It is still a man's world, and at first the woods are dominated by male voices.

But soon even that will change as Americans of both sexes begin to find in nature itself an outlet for the release of tensions created by the new pace of life.

Socoteau River, Maine, c. 1885 Joseph J. Kirkbride

There are other outlets as well. On summer evenings, for example, the circus brings to the countryside countless wonders to delight the eye and intrigue the mind. The circus features games of skill and chance; trapeze artists from Italy, lions from Africa, elephants from India.

New Bedford, Massachusetts, c. 1900   Albert Cook Church

New Haven, Connecticut, 1907 T. S. Bronson

"Each year," writes a Midwestern farm boy, "the circus comes along from the East, trailing clouds of glorified dust and filling our minds with the color of romance."

Oak Bluffs, Massachusetts, c. 1875   Richard C. Woodard

Beyond the circus another kind of romance is apparent. More free time leads to new ways of courtship. Games that bring men and women together — in a proper way, of course — become popular.

One is the ideal game: sociable, yet contemplative; orderly, yet full of excitement. The popularity of croquet is unprecedented and manufacturers offer wickets with special candleholders so that the game can be played at night. "Young ladies are fond of cheating at this game," states one early rule book, "but they do so only because they think men like it." The sex of the author is not given.

Games are played everywhere — in
backyards, city streets, neighborhood
parks — and encourage competition,
cooperation, and fortitude. Indoors and
outdoors, there is a new emphasis on
physical fitness.

Wellesley, Massachusetts, 1893   Photographer unknown

Most important is a game played with ash and horsehide. It is baseball, and as early as 1872 it is called "the national pastime." Its origins are obscure. Some say it began in England; others cite colonial America.

A man named Abner Doubleday is often given credit. By the turn of the century it is clear that, whatever its origins, it has become purely American.

Baseball is the game of games, and it comes free of guilt. An American cardinal — from the Church, not St. Louis — pronounces it holy and healthy. On summer afternoons the stadium, the corner lot, the open field are all transformed into places of epic adventure by eighteen men, a bat, and a ball.

New Haven, Connecticut, 1908   T. S. Bronson

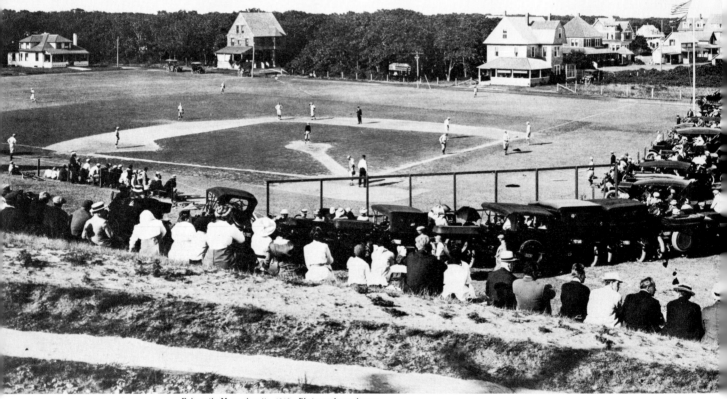

Falmouth, Massachusetts, 1910   Photographer unknown

St. Louis, Missouri, c. 1910   Photographer unknown

The rich man's yacht fighting the seas cannot compete with the skill of the hook slide, the beauty of the shoestring catch, the grace of the double play. By 1899 there are two major leagues at play, and in 1903 the Boston Americans beat the Pittsburgh Nationals in the first World Series. "Baseball," says Mark Twain, "is the very symbol, the outward and visible expression of the drive and pride and rush and struggle of the raging, tearing, booming nineteenth century." It is the supreme game in a nation just learning to play.

By 1900 new forms of recreation and amusement are springing up all over America. In addition to sports and games, there are the theater, the automobile, the camera — more and more ways to spend time away from the job. Many of those who are not playing are watching, for the new emphasis on play brings about a major new phenomenon in American life — the spectator.

Overleaf: Barnstable, Massachusetts, c. 1900; Edward Sprague

College football is particularly popular.
From coast to coast, men, women, and
children pack together on a Saturday
afternoon to watch young men give
their hearts and their blood for alma
mater and manhood.

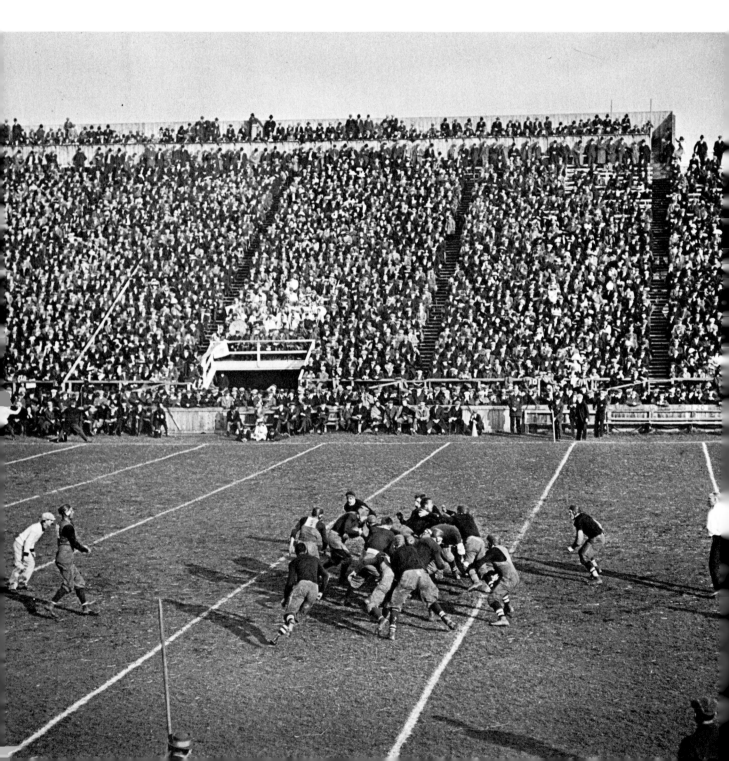

On the sea, steam vessels are jammed
to overflowing as spectators flock to the
finish lines of yachting matches, cup
races, and regattas. Americans are not
only finding joy in playing; everywhere
they are finding joy in watching as well.

Newport, Rhode Island, c. 1895   N. L. Stebbins

Oak Bluffs, Massachusetts, c. 1895   Photographer unknown

"Where is the place the Sabbath is not losing ground?" asks a discouraged reformer. "To the mass of the working men," he says, "Sunday is no more than a holiday . . . an excuse for excursions, saloons, baseball games, and carousels."

He is right. Day by day Americans are learning the value of relaxation as their labors are made intense by the factory and the assembly line, the machine and the mill. Play, they are discovering, is not so much a rejection of God as it is an embracement of life. It is an admission that there can be joy outside of work, enrichment in amusement. Enrichment — and profit. It is not long before some Americans begin to see that one man's play is another man's opportunity. Play and recreation can become big business. Amusement parks are the first Newports of the working class.

In Boston there is Paragon Park with its roller coaster. In Hoboken there is Elysian Fields with bear dances and picnics. San Francisco has "The Chutes," and, of course, there is Coney Island in New York.

"There are a great many people here," says one visitor to Elysian Fields, "male and female, but," he adds, "few respectable ones." When your week has been burdened with the "respectability" of the sweatshop or assembly line, however, it is a quality you are most willing to lose on the Whip, the Bump, the Super Loop, or the Helter Skelter.

Coney Island, New York, c. 1900 Detroit Publishing Company

SPIRAL DIP

Salisbury Beach, Massachusetts, c. 1910   Photographer unknown

Chicago, Illinois, c. 1900   W. Taylor

Other ways out of the city may be found as well. You can walk the deck of an excursion steamer and travel up the Hudson or down the Mississippi, along the coast of Lake Michigan, through San Francisco Bay or across Cape Cod Bay to Provincetown.

The band plays. The air is fresh and cool. The company is good. A picnic lunch and a one-dollar round-trip fare give you the chance to play like the rich. You sit back; you relax and, for a moment, forget the heat, the stale air, and the congestion of the city.

Newport, Rhode Island, 1899   Photographer unknown

Trains, which have become the long-distance haulers of people and freight, can also be used for joyful excursions. And, for those who can afford it, there is, of course, the automobile. By the first decade of the new century, a day's outing by car is one of life's real pleasures.

Milford, Connecticut, 1908   T. S. Bronson

The very duration of playtime is changing. No longer is it restricted to the early evening or even the weekend. The ever-growing American middle class has discovered a new phenomenon — the one- and sometimes two-week vacation. New types of amusement are created that can hold one's attention for long stretches of time. Many people, for example, can now travel to the World's Fairs, which, at the turn of the century, begin to compete for the attention of Americans in every part of the nation.

Chicago, Illinois, 1893   Photographer unknown

Each of these fairs offers its own special forms of play. At the Pan-American Exposition there is "a trip to the moon." At the World's Columbian Exposition in Chicago there is the wondrous White City and George Ferris's giant revolving wheel. It is two hundred sixty-four feet high. Each car holds sixty passengers. Twenty-seven million Americans pass through the gates of the Columbian Exposition — to marvel, to wonder, and to play.

Chicago, Illinois, 1893   Photographer unknown

There are World's Fairs in St. Louis, in Buffalo, in San Francisco. Each offers its own visions: of life as it is lived around the world, of life as it will be lived in America in years to come. The World's Fairs bring men, women, and children to the cities to learn as well as to be entertained.

Chicago, Illinois, 1893   Photographer unknown

Palm Beach, Florida, c. 1905   Detroit Publishing Company

Beyond the cities is the shore. Now that
they have learned how to play, Americans rediscover the sea with its white
beaches, cool breezes, blue waters. The
shore itself asks to be enjoyed. If bat
and ball, roller coaster and merry-go-
round are not enough, then there is
much to be said for the delights of sand
and surf.

Atlantic City, New Jersey, 1897   W. B. Davidson

Not all that is said is positive. The beach has long been looked upon with suspicion. Modesty and concerns about health have kept most Americans from full enjoyment of the water. "We look with alarm," states one early magazine, "upon the growing practice of exposing one's complexion to the harmful rays of the sun." There are also serious fears concerning the moral dangers inherent in the possibility that men and women might swim together in the same ocean.

New Haven, Connecticut, 1906   T. S. Bronson

Coney Island, New York, c. 1895   Detroit Publishing Company

At first beaches are observed rather carefully from a distance. Bathing is confined to the young and the "foolish." But times are changing, and the cool waters are hard to resist.

Increasingly the lake and ocean shores are filled with people. They come to swim, to sail, to be refreshed by the breezes. By 1900 play in sand and surf is widely accepted. In fact, the beach has become America's favorite summer playground.

New Haven, Connecticut, 1906   T. S. Bronson

Atlantic City, New Jersey, 1907   T. S. Bronson

Finally it is all combined — the amusement park, the beach, the playing fields, nature itself — into a new phenomenon of recreation called the resort. The buildings are large and luxurious; the air is fresh and clean; the scenery is often spectacular; the food is abundant and good. Here all of the era's new-found joys are housed in one locale.

Resorts spring up all over America — in the mountains, beside the lakes, at the ocean. A nation that for so long has felt guilty about play now has very temples of play in which to relax.

Lake George, New York, 1889   S. R. Stoddard

"What shall we do with our leisure once we have it?" President Garfield asked. By the turn of the century Americans are supplying many answers. They have come a long way from the front porch. The ball field, the amusement park, the woods, the lakes, the beaches, the resorts are filled. Recreation has become a permanent part of the nation's life. Americans have not only learned to play, they have learned to enjoy it as well.

Raquette Lake, New York, 1889   S. R. Stoddard

Bretton Woods, New Hampshire, c. 1910   N. L. Stebbins

THE AMERICAN FAMILY ALBUM

Pictures from the American family album.

Portland, Oregon, 1894   Worthington Cornell

Pictures are taken by cameras of every description as the photograph becomes a family treasure and everyone becomes a photographer.

Knoxville, Tennessee, c. 1900   Photographer unknown

Memories of home and family are preserved in albums and displayed proudly in living rooms from coast to coast.

Ohio, 1897   Worthington Cornell

At the turn of the century it is the American family that best expresses the hopes and realities of the nation. While industry redefines the economy and science reworks the universe, home and the family remain the symbols of the nation's values and stability.

Kansas City, Kansas, 1893   S. D. Roberts

In every region of the country, at every level of society, the sanctity of family life is a notion that is held close to the heart and expressed daily in a multitude of ways.

Custer County, Nebraska, c. 1890   Solomon Butcher

It is no accident that the song "Home Sweet Home" is one of the most popular ballads of the day. It is not by chance that schoolchildren across the nation open their *McGuffey's Reader* and warmly recite: "We are all here! Father, Mother, Sister, Brother, / All who hold each other dear."

The line could well be extended to include grandmother, grandfather, and maiden aunt as well, for at the turn of the century they too are an important part of the family unit.

Location unknown, c. 1895   Worthington Cornell

196

At the center of family life is the homestead itself. Most typically it is a two-story wooden structure with six to eight rooms. It is heated by coal stoves, lighted by kerosene lamps. Off the front hall are the living room and the seldom-used formal parlor.

Western Massachusetts, c. 1900   George and Alvah Howes

"It is true," recalls one author, "that our parlor was excessively formal. Yet I cannot say that I remember it without respect. It was, after all, where my mother entertained company; where my sisters had their birthday parties; . . . where our Christmas tree stood, . . . and where my mother, at last, was laid in her coffin."

New Haven, Connecticut, 1906   T. S. Bronson

The pride of many houses is the front
porch, complete with gliders, sofas, and
chairs. It is a favorite spot in which to
relax, to visit with friends or relatives,
or simply to watch the world go by.

Location unknown, c. 1890   Photographer unknown

Backyards are important, too. They
contain barns, woodsheds, gardens,
often a well for drinking water, and the
family privy.

Portland, Oregon, 1894   Worthington Cornell

Photographers in every region of the country find profit in taking pictures of families posed proudly in front of their homes, for the record of generations is vitally important. The life expectancy of a male born in 1880 is just over forty-three years. More than three hundred thousand Americans die each year from influenza, pneumonia, or tuberculosis. No wonder so many parents outlive their children. No wonder a family photograph is so deeply cherished.

Western Massachusetts, c. 1900   George and Alvah Howes

Included in the pictures are the family's most treasured possessions — sewing machines, bicycles, horses, buggies, the family pet.

"The photographer was coming," recalls a schoolgirl, "and for a full week we argued over what we would place in front of the house. You can imagine my brother's disappointment when, on the day of the picture, Father changed his mind and forbade him to bring his goat."

At the turn of the century the home is the center of calm in a world of change. It is the place where tradition is still important, where roles are clearly defined. For most people it is the one spot where one can be secure. A young Henry Ford speaks for millions of Americans when he recalls, "More than once I heard Mother say, if we couldn't be happy here in this house, we'd never be happy anywhere else."

There is a prescribed role for each member of the family. The roles have long been ordained. "The relative positions assumed by men and women in our civilization," says Grover Cleveland, "were assigned long ago by a higher intelligence than ours."

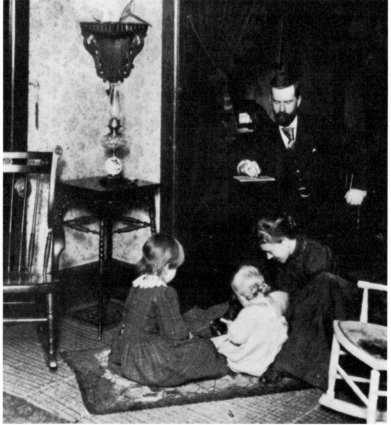

Portland, Oregon, c. 1895   Photographer unknown

For men the "higher intelligence" has created a world of variety, challenge and invention. It is men who run the businesses, cast the votes, shape the nation.

From New York to San Francisco, on the prairie and in the Rockies, for pioneer and Easterner, farmer or shopkeeper, doctor or railroad worker, it is the same. Men are the breadwinners. Women work in the home.

Boston, Massachusetts, c. 1900   Worthington Cornell

Detroit, Michigan, 1896   Photographer unknown

It is truly a man's world. There are scores of places that are exclusively masculine: the club, the band, the volunteer fire department, the neighborhood sporting association, the barbershop.

Junction City, Kansas, c. 1900   Joseph Pennell

Junction City, Kansas, c. 1900 Joseph Pennell

And there is the saloon. In 1900 some three thousand breweries and distilleries across the nation supply more than one hundred thousand saloons. One newspaper reports that in the cities of Boston and Chicago half of the male population visits a saloon at least once a day. At the turn of the century the neighborhood bar is the very epitome of the manly retreat.

"There is something enervating in feminine companionship," states *Cosmopolitan* magazine. "The genuine man feels that he must go off alone or with other men, out in the open air, roughing it among the rough, as a mental tonic."

Hunting clubs, fishing clubs, marching societies, fraternal organizations all across the country provide Father with ample opportunity to be a "genuine man."

Overleaf: Newport, Rhode Island, c. 1895; photographer unknown

And what about Mother? Her life is very different. The worlds of men and women are separated at the front door. They are as different from each other as the sexes.

A woman's domain is the home. Her job is to take care of it — a job that occupies almost all her waking hours. There are no processed foods. Nearly everything must be made from scratch.

Lynn, Massachusetts, 1895   Frances Benjamin Johnston

There are still relatively few labor-saving devices for the house. While Father runs the machine or manages the business, Mother prepares the food, scrubs the floor, watches after the children, does the ironing, hangs out the clothes.

It is no wonder that few women find amusement in a couplet of the day that states, "Here lies a poor woman who was always tired; / She lived in a house where help was not hired."

Chicago, Illinois, 1896   Photographer unknown

213

Lancaster, Massachusetts, c. 1890   J. A. Macdonald

Despite the long days and the tedious work, many middle-class American women do find time away from their chores. Their leisure time is spent much differently from that of men, yet it is leisure time nonetheless. Women gather at the horticultural society, the library league, the sewing bee, the afternoon tea. These are genteel diversions, yet important parts of a woman's world.

214

Black River Falls, Wisconsin, c. 1890   Charles Van Schaick

Cornwall, Connecticut, 1906   T. S. Bronson

It is an unequal world, there is no question about that. But women are not totally powerless. Says one visitor to the United States, "The American woman may not have the vote, but she has other means of getting her way. The women here, starting with the youngest, are the best looking and best dressed I have ever encountered. What's more, they know how attractive they are and they don't hesitate to use this fact to their advantage."

Kansas City, Kansas, 1893   S. D. Roberts

217

At the turn of the century an abundance of books and magazines offer advice to women on how they may indeed get their way. Romantic stories feature demure but determined women. Magazine articles describe how the ideal can be attained.

Los Angeles, California, 1895   Worthington Cornell

Location unknown, c. 1896. Photographer unknown.

The magazines are filled with advice on dress and fashion. For middle-class American women, the rules of dress are extremely exacting. If they are to be perceived as soft and lovely, then they must dress the part. They must look like hourglasses. In order to accomplish this they spend over fourteen million dollars a year on corsets alone.

Hats are very important as well. No respectable woman thinks of stepping outdoors without one. Many of the hats are truly spectacular, festooned with ribbons, bows, and buttons, and feathers from almost every bird that flies.

Washington, D.C., 1903 Frances Benjamin Johnston

New Haven, Connecticut, 1906   T. S. Bronson

Jacksonville, Florida, c. 1900   Photographer unknown

For men, too, dress is of the greatest significance. Even if a man is not a policeman, a fireman, or a railroad engineer, he still has a uniform.

A stiff collar, a well-ironed shirt, necktie, suit, vest, pocket watch, hat — these are symbols of a man's world in a time when, above all else, dress emphasizes the difference between the sexes.

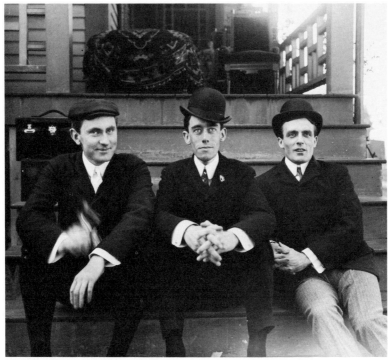

Cleveland, Ohio, 1897   Worthington Cornell

Location unknown, c. 1895   Photographer unknown

Ogdensburg, New York, c. 1905   Edgar A. Mearns

The emphasis on appearance affects the
children as well. They are presented to
the world as they are expected to be:
scrubbed, polished, knowing their
proper place.

Yet the actual day-to-day life of middle-class American children is not so formal. States one foreign observer, "American parents make a great deal of fuss about their children in public but in truth they leave them pretty much to their own devices. That is, as long as they do not disturb the daily routine of the household."

The American family at the turn of the
century: rigidly structured, precise in its
roles,

Medford, Massachusetts, 1899   Worthington Cornell

and, like everything else, about to
change.

Columbus, Ohio, 1897 Worthington Cornell

At the beginning of the era it is hard to imagine a time when young men and women will seek their place in the world outside of the family. It is difficult to believe that security can seem stifling, that planned futures can be perceived as oppressive. But as the world outside the home is swept by change, the family itself is transformed.

It takes place first on the farm. Farming is uncertain and the family can be broken by circumstances over which no one has control — vagaries of weather, crop failure, drastic fluctuations in prices. When the land cannot support a father's dreams, then sons and daughters are forced to pursue dreams of their own in other places.

How does it happen? The churches have taught them to honor their father and mother, to love God and country, to love home. In school they have learned more than to read and write, add and multiply. There too the emphasis has been on God and country, home and hygiene.

Location unknown, c. 1910   Photographer unknown

Now many of them are leaving to find new places. They are building a way of life for themselves and adopting new values. Where have they learned to do this? Who has taught them? The answer is in the times themselves. Newspapers, magazines, dime novels, mail-order catalogues have created a new awareness and a desire to be independent, to be part of a changing world, a world filled with new opportunities.

Cleveland, Ohio, 1897   Worthington Cornell

Fond Du Lac, Wisconsin, c. 1900   William A. Titus

For women the changes are especially dramatic. As the nation's economy continues to grow it becomes apparent that women are actually needed in the business world. The growth of American industry has created a tide of paperwork, and inventions like the typewriter and the adding machine have provided the means by which to deal with the problem. Male office workers consider that use of the new machines is beneath them. Not so the women. For unmarried women, office work is a way out of depending upon fathers and brothers for financial support. It is also a way to meet new people and create a life of one's own.

New York City, c. 1910   Barre News Service

234

There are changes for married women too. The newspapers and magazines are filled with more to read than simply fashion news or the latest romance.

There are stories of women campaigning for the vote, stories of women working for causes much more far-reaching than that of the horticultural society or the library league.

New York City, c. 1910   Barre News Service

Pictures from the American family album, taken at the turn of the century.

Middletown, Connecticut, 1907   T. S. Bronson

Fathers, mothers, sisters, brothers.   All who hold each other dear.

Lancaster, Massachusetts, c. 1890   J. A. Macdonald

VISIONS OF AMERICA

The turn of the century. For the majority of Americans it is still a time of incredible promise. It is still an age of unabashed confidence.

"We seek no other paths," a United States senator says, "than those we first followed. In accomplishment . . . in courage . . . in art . . . we find nothing to recall us from the course of our fathers."

Location unknown, c. 1905   Detroit Publishing Company

The "course of our fathers" is the means to progress. It is the way to new paths, new worlds, to all the good that man can do on earth.

As new paths are found, others begin to be forgotten. New means to new ends leave old ways behind, and with them cultures, life-styles, values begin to disappear as well. There is no permanence in the "course of our fathers"; only change.

There is, however, a growing permanent record of the era. It is being put together by photographers in cities and towns all across America. Most of these cameramen and -women stick close to home. They photograph what they know best: their friends, their relatives, their own locale. Most are unaware that together they are compiling a lasting visual document of their time.

West New Portland, Maine, c. 1900   Chansonetta Emmons

Location unknown, c. 1910 Photographer unknown

Technical improvements have made photography simpler, easier, and more accessible to amateurs. Professionals still use tripods, but hand-held cameras are becoming increasingly popular. Flexible film has been invented. Large photographic houses are now in business to develop and print one's pictures.

Still, it is the photographer, not the equipment, that is most important, and it is the photographer's eye that chooses what will finally be recorded. Most photographers take pictures for the sheer pleasure of it, yet they see their subjects from their own unique perspective, with their own vision.

Manchester, New Hampshire, c. 1900 Ulrich Bourgeois

There is, for example, a photographer in Kingfield, Maine — a hamlet comprised of eight hundred people, most of them descendants of the town's founder, Squire Solomon Stanley. The days are long in Kingfield. Men and women work from dawn until dusk. They have names like Hannah and Tristam, Aunt Lucy and Emery.

The men farm the land and work in mills run by waterpower. They make wheelbarrows and ax handles, wooden rakes and sap buckets.

There is a saying in Kingfield: If you throw an apple you are sure to hit a Stanley. One of the Stanleys you are most apt to hit is a woman with the uncommon name of Chansonetta. In 1900 Chansonetta Stanley Emmons is a widow, a mother, a trained artist, and a photographer — a photographer who is either a friend or a relative of almost everyone in Kingfield and the adjoining village of West New Portland. With her camera she will record whole generations of her neighbors and kinfolk.

She approaches her photography as art. She uses only natural light, even for interior shots. She composes each picture as artistically as possible. Hers is a special talent, the ability to make a personal statement about each of the subjects she knows so well. She is a documentary photographer with the eye of an artist.

Her twin brothers F. E. and F. O. Stanley have been pioneers in the development of the dry glass-plate process. It is while they are perfecting this process that she becomes interested in photography. Her brothers will amass a respectable fortune in their photographic business. Later they will become more famous, for they will invent a brand-new type of automobile, the Stanley Steamer. The brothers are generous to Chansonetta. After the death of her husband they see to it that she is well cared for financially. She can devote most of her time to photography. She repays their generosity with photographs that touch the mind and the heart as well as the eye.

Her pictures show people at both ends of the spectrum of life, for she has a way with both old folks and children. She makes them feel at ease. Through her camera the elders are preserved in penetrating and incisive images. These are individuals whose lives are anchored in the rocky Maine soil. Chansonetta captures them with all the common trappings of their way of life: the table chair, the inside well, the grinder, the spinning wheel. She records these people at their daily routines with a dignity and sensitivity worthy of the subjects.

Kingfield, Maine, 1901   Chansonetta Emmons

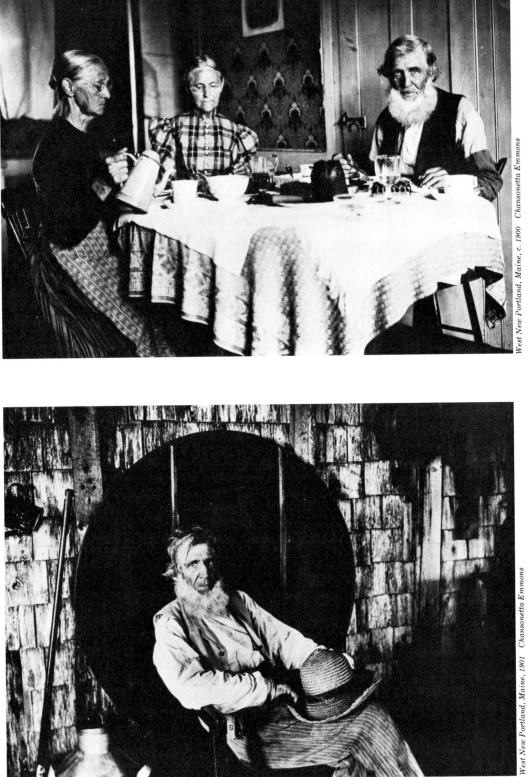

West New Portland, Maine, c. 1900   Chansonetta Emmons

West New Portland, Maine, 1901   Chansonetta Emmons

Franklin County, Maine, c. 1905 Chansonetta Emmons

West New Portland, Maine, c. 1910 Chansonetta Emmons

247

Newton, Massachusetts, c. 1905   Chansonetta Emmons

Kingfield, Maine, c. 1905   Chansonetta Emmons

She takes particular pleasure in photographing the children, and her pictures are a delight to the eye. She has a special ability to capture the simplicity, the humor, and the innocence of children. Who could imagine that these boys will fight in a global war; that these girls will try to keep their families together through a great depression?

Chansonetta Stanley Emmons has a purpose and a vision. She sees a unique image of America and on glass plates made by her own brothers she freezes what she sees, preserving glimpses of a way of life that future generations of photographers will not find.

Kingfield, Maine, 1901 Chansonetta Emmons

Chansonetta Emmons takes her pictures of people in the northeastern corner of the United States. A full continent away there is another group of people and another way of life that is about to become only a memory. They are found in the Pacific Northwest, a land of giant forests of fir, cedar, and redwood trees: trees with which to build the homes, offices, and cities of America.

Into these forests come the men who risk their lives to fell these trees. They saw them into logs, haul the logs to sawmills, and turn the logs into lumber. It is a rough business, carried out by rough men — for a dollar a day. Into these woods comes Darius Kinsey, a photographer. Along with his wife he has a successful commercial studio near Seattle, but he sees another opportunity for profit in the logging camps.

The lumberjacks are isolated in their camps for months at a time. Surely they will be willing — even eager — to spend fifty cents for a photograph of themselves beside one of the giant trees they have come to conquer: a photograph to send to a mother or a wife or a sweetheart; a photograph perhaps to prove to a man that he really does exist in the midst of this wilderness of trees.

Washington State, c. 1910 Darius Kinsey

Lake Cavanaugh, Washington, c. 1905   Darius Kinsey

253

Darius Kinsey is barely five feet tall, yet he will spend a major part of his life photographing the tallest growing things on earth. He is particularly fascinated by the loggers — their toil, their tools, their courage. He is determined to spend as much time among them as possible.

Kinsey is endowed with incredible energy. He rises at four o'clock each morning. He is at a camp by five. He has cameras of every description, including one that handles huge twenty-by-twenty-four-inch plates. He hires youngsters to carry the enormous planks and the fifty-gallon drums he uses to build platforms upon which to stand in order to get high enough to take his pictures. Few youngsters will work for him more than once. The task is much too hard.

He is a religious man, a devout Methodist. His business cards carry a slogan: "We will photograph anything, anywhere, anytime, except on Sunday." His purpose turns into a passion. He spends more and more time with the men in the forest. The task of developing the negatives and shipping the mounted prints to the camps falls to his wife. For her, too, the job of recording a vanishing way of labor becomes a full-time occupation. The loggers, though suspicious by nature, come to respect Kinsey and his work. They look forward to his visits. He eats alongside sawyers and fullers, haulers and skidders. Soon he has another slogan. "You aren't a logger," it reads, "until you own a dollar watch and have your photograph taken beside a tree by Kinsey."

Photographs by Kinsey become as much a part of the logging camps as the men, the axes, the saws, the horses, the heavy equipment. They are taken by a perfectionist — a man who will spend as long as is necessary to get the proper light, the proper pose. Each print is developed by sixteen separate washings to ensure that it will not fade.

For more than fifty years Darius Kinsey travels from camp to camp. He documents every aspect of the logging operation. He records generations of lumbermen who show in their faces the hardship of their labor, and pride in the knowledge that they are conquering a wilderness.

Snoqualmie, Washington, c. 1900 Darius Kinsey

The photographs reveal something else as well, for they are pictures of a way of life that is destroying itself. Each day the trees fall, not to be replaced. Kinsey captures images of men unwittingly working themselves out of jobs.

After fifty years of photographing lumberjacks and their work, Darius Kinsey dies of a fall from a giant redwood stump, a man who literally gives his life documenting a way of work that will soon vanish.

Washington State, c. 1900   Darius Kinsey

Meanwhile, in still another part of
America, another photographer begins
to make another kind of photographic
record, a chronicle of what will become
the most romantic figure in all of American
history: the American cowboy. A
legend in his own time, bigger than life,
celebrated in song and story, the cowboy
is a man in love with freedom, taming
one of the last frontiers.

Texas, c. 1905   Erwin Smith

The photographer's name is Erwin Smith. At the age of eight he visits his uncle's ranch in Bonham, Texas. He falls in love with the ranch, the range, and the men who work the herds. Summers he returns to Bonham and the love affair grows deeper. Smith is a talented young man. He can draw; he can paint; he can sculpture. He decides to celebrate the life of the American cowboy in statuary. At the age of eighteen he goes to Chicago to study with one of the nation's leading sculptors. At the age of twenty he prepares to go to Boston to continue his education, but he realizes that if he waits any longer to return to the range, there will be nothing left to sculpture. "I know that life won't wait," he says, "and the technique will."

Texas, c. 1905 Erwin Smith

He is right. Already much of the open range has disappeared. Growing numbers of farms and sodbuster settlements are forcing more and more ranchers to fence in their land. Instead of going to Boston, Smith returns to Texas armed with a camera, which he straps to his horse next to his bedroll and his saddle. He works alongside the cowpunchers, gaining their respect, their confidence, and their cooperation. At night he draws sketches of the scenes he hopes to photograph the next day, for he knows that such scenes can hardly be posed. He has a particular ability to arrest action. Rearing horses, men and beasts on the gallop, lassos flying through the air — he captures the motion and the activity that are the trademarks of life on the range and the ranch.

He knows the work, he loves the life, and it shows. It shows in the faces of the men. It shows in the pictures he takes of the cattle drives, the roundups, the brandings, the chuckwagons, the campfires.

Erwin Smith leaves a remarkable legacy, a chronicle of the American cowboys as they really were. It is all there: the strain, the hard work, and the dust — always the dust. Unlike the Hollywood versions that are to come later, Smith's cowboys are men with a job to do. They do it well.

Texas, c. 1905   Erwin Smith

Texas, c. 1905   Erwin Smith

Mobile, Alabama, 1906 Detroit Publishing Company

As Smith is chronicling his cowboys, and Darius Kinsey recording his lumberjacks, and Chansonetta Emmons immortalizing her kinfolk and neighbors, an entire photographic company is formed. It is called the Detroit Publishing Company and it is founded by two men. One of them is one of America's best-known photographers, William Henry Jackson. He has gained much fame as America's premier frontier photographer. His pictures of the West, particularly those of the Yellowstone region, are among the most spectacular ever taken. They are so powerful, in fact, that it is a portfolio of these photographs, circulated among the members of the United States Congress, that leads to the establishment of Yellowstone as the nation's first national park.

Jackson forms the Detroit Publishing Company with a man named William Livingston. They send photographers across the length and breadth of the nation. They weave a visual tapestry of America, as complete a portrait of the nation as has ever been made. Jackson himself takes many of the photographs. A brilliant Boston cameraman named Henry Peabody takes thousands more. The names of countless others in the company's employ will unfortunately remain unknown.

The company's photographers are armed with the best equipment possible. Improvements in transportation facilities allow them to get to more places with more equipment than ever before. A visual record can be made of each region — its people, its work, its play — at a time when so much is changing. Change itself can be documented through the eye of the camera.

Detroit Company photographers capture the flavor of small-town America: Fort Thomas, Kentucky; Baribou River, Wisconsin; Santa Barbara, California; Chattanooga, Tennessee; Mobile, Alabama — quiet communities, poised on the edge of change.

Most striking perhaps are the pictures of the cities, busy, bustling, growing — New York, Chicago, Boston, Detroit, San Francisco, Providence — the very symbols of change in turn-of-the-century America.

A coast-to-coast record of work is made. It reveals the immense diversity of labor in this remarkable country, and shows grape pickers in California, shipbuilders in Chicago, tobacco workers in Kentucky, street vendors in New York, policemen in St. Louis, steelworkers in Birmingham, fishermen in San Francisco, railroad men in Los Angeles, merchants in Boston, miners in Pennsylvania, dockworkers in busy ports everywhere.

Birmingham, Alabama, 1906   Detroit Publishing Company

Memphis, Tennessee, 1906   Detroit Publishing Company

The Detroit Publishing Company photographers document every state in the
nation and reveal the remarkable variety in the American landscape.

Tucson, Arizona, c. 1900   Detroit Publishing Company

But most of all, their pictures show the people: people at work, at play, on the move; black and white; rich and poor. The American people.

Location unknown, c. 1900   Detroit Publishing Company